MW00582290

To: DaQuan

From:

Thank you ♡

AFTER THE NEST

The Culinary Edition

Antoinette L. Beeks

Antoinette L. Beeks © 2021

All rights reserved. No part of this book may be reproduced, stored, or transmitted by any means- whether auditory, graphic, mechanical, or electronic- without written permission of both publisher and author, except in the case of brief excerpts used in critical articles and certain other noncommercial uses permitted by copyright law. Unauthorized reproduction of any part of this work is illegal and is punishable by law.

ISBN: 978-0-578-33365-6

Because of the dynamic nature of the internet, any web addresses or links contained in this book may have changed since publication and may no longer be valid. The views expressed in this work are solely those of the author and do not necessarily reflect the views of the publisher, and the publisher disclaims any responsibility for them.

Printed in the United States of America

Book Design by Brand It Beautifully™ @ www.branditbeautifully.com

Food Photos courtesy of Andrea Lynn Bynum

Script quotations from The Authorized (King James) Version unless otherwise noted. Rights in the Authorized Version in the United Kingdom are vested in the Crown. Reproduced by permission of the Crown's patentee, Cambridge University Press.

Disclaimer:
Consult with your physician prior to following any
meal plan or changes in diet.

Dear friend, I hope all is well with you and that you are as healthy in body as you are strong in spirit.

— 3 John 1:2

TABLE OF CONTENTS

DEDICATION

You are the foundation of my approach to food, even before I knew the value and meaning of it.

Grandma Ezell,
You inspired me at an early age to eat straight from the farm.

Momma Dorothea,
You inspired me to cook and cook well. Thank you for expanding my palate.

To my favorite girl and favorite chef, Aunt Gloria,
Many thanks to you and Dawn for being patient and walking me through the SOS cooking calls **After the Nest**.

INTRODUCTION

Welcome to *After the Nest!*

After the Nest is a tool to help young adults break through the fear and anxiety of cooking.

What's in it for you?
- Empowerment to be your own chef
- Learning to create simple yet delicious meals
- A focus on fun and discovery, less on results
- Learning to eat to thrive
- Building a kitchen space around your personality
- A return on investment for your mind and body
- Opportunity to learn from my blunders and challenges

What's in it for me?
- The joy in helping young adults create a sustainable cooking lifestyle.

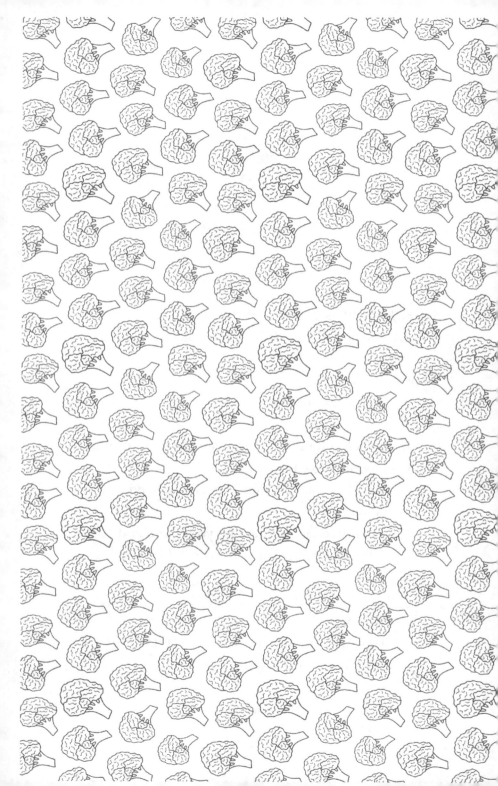

CHAPTER I
The Deep. Fried. Liver

LIVER, GRAVY, ONIONS, and mash potatoes were on the menu. I was nervous, yet excited because this was my first-time cooking. I just knew it would taste like home. After buying my groceries, I prepped the ingredients and was ready to burn (while "burn" is slang for cooking well, in this case it's literal).

I watched it sink into the abyss of cold, viscous grease. That unseasoned, heavily floured liver. Wait! I had forgotten to heat the oil. Uggh!! "I can fix this," I said. "I'll just turn the burner alllll the way up high and cover the pan. That should work", I convinced myself.

There was a long, eerie pause. Then... BOOM. A Mount Vesuvius eruption of grease and liver everywhere. I hustled to rescue the liver, while simultaneously calming the raging fire alarm.

After the smoke cleared, I plated the blackened liver next to the boxed mashed potatoes, no gravy. Fork and knife in hand, I hesitantly made the first cut. "Incision" is a more fitting word. This incision produced what could be described as a mini crime scene on a plate. As I dry heaved over dinner, I knew in that moment, I was going to starve to death.

(Cue dramatic music).

Why didn't I watch and learn from my mother, grandmother, and aunt, all of whom are fabulous cooks, as they prepared heaven "scent" meals, one of which I am struggling to recreate? "Why is this happening to me?" I questioned God.

Being in this vulnerable space cultivated resiliency. Yes, dinner was wrecked, but I learned what NOT to do. And so can you.

As Nestlings, we relied on caregivers for nourishment while in the nest. Nestlings are baby birds that receive daily meals delivered directly to their hungry, gaping mouths.

The Nestling develops into a Fledgling, outgrowing the nest and venturing out on its own. In order to survive, it must learn how to acquire its own food.

Now that you're out on your own, you face a similar challenge to that baby bird. You may be scrambling (pun intended, you'll see a few of these) to answer the million-dollar question: **How will I eat?**

The question following that is probably: Can I order it?

But the most important question you'll ever ask yourself: **Can I cook it?**

The answer: **Of course you can!**

▶ *The Takeaway:*

- Accept mistakes because they'll happen
- Be confident enough to try
- Celebrate all wins (making a salad is a win)

Let's talk about the benefits of cooking your own meals.

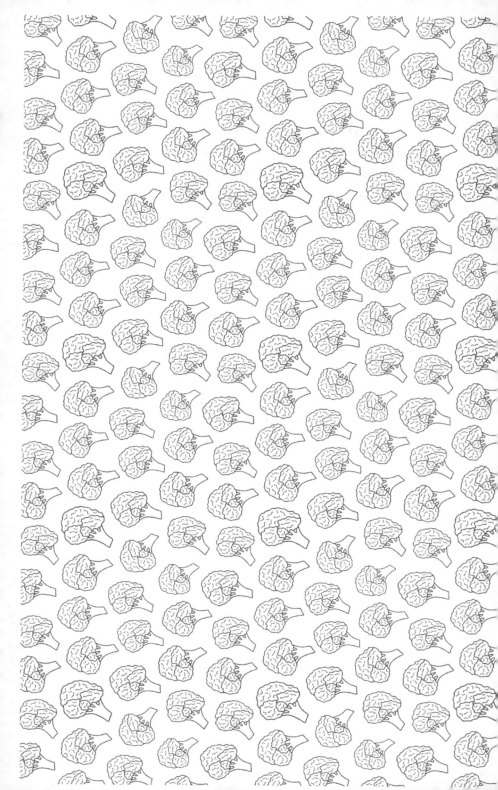

CHAPTER 2

Benefits of Cooking Your Own Meal

I DIDN'T REALIZE the benefits of cooking until I... um... actually started cooking.

▶ Benefit #1: You're in control

In a world with staggering rates of what I call "Fork & Spoon" diseases (obesity, high blood pressure, diabetes, heart disease), you have the opportunity to develop a strategy against them.

Let's use dining out for example. Even though you pick food from a menu, the restaurant ultimately decides what goes into that food. Whether it's extra sugar, extra salt, or extra fat, you are no longer in control. When you cook for yourself, you have a choice in what ingredients and how much of each ingredient goes into your body.

▶ Benefit #2: Eat what you like

I encourage my clients to prepare foods they enjoy eating. If there is one particular food that you absolutely adored growing up, cook that. If there is one you completely abhor and were forced to eat as a kid, find an alternative that provides similar benefits. Or find a way to spruce that food up to your liking.

For instance, some people despise tomatoes or cannot stomach the acidity it brings. As a result, they may avoid it at all costs – but the tomato offers a host of nutrients. So how do you ensure you are not depriving your body of the necessary vitamins and minerals a particular food offers?

To start, apply what you already know about that food. Most tomatoes are red. Color is an indicator of the nutrients a whole food contains. Second, find a substitute that has a similar color.

Research your food to learn the nutrients they contain. This allows you to be more decisive in your substitution.

▶ Benefit #3: Self-care

If I told you cooking is a form of self-care, would you believe me? Your kitchen can provide a safe space to relax and deep breathe as you chop, dice, or sauté. You'd be surprised how much aggression you can take out on a mixing bowl.

The cooking process also creates bonding moments with friends and loved ones. If you're an introvert like me, cooking can bring out the talker in you and help you feel more relaxed around people you've just met.

▶ Benefit #4: Money for other stuff

Depending on where you live in the world, the average cost of a burger, fries, and drink can be anywhere from $8 - 15. Dining out for meals like this multiple times a day each week can quickly add up. That's over $400 a month.

Guilty as charged. As an undergrad and also *After the Nest*, I maxed out my credit card and went into debt purchasing fast food. Can you believe that? Deep down, I was unmotivated, but the root of it all was that I was afraid to approach the subject of cooking. I felt lost and inadequate in the kitchen. Defeated, broke, and unhealthy, I knew I had to do something - and fast. I did what I'm about to share with you.

Each time you dine out:

1.　Hold on to your receipt (or take a pic of it).

2.　At the end of the week, collect those receipts.

3.　Calculate the total amount spent eating out for the week.

4.　Multiply that amount by 4 to calculate your average monthly dining out expense.

Once you have this data, create a financial strategy that works best for you. For example:

- If you dine out 8 times a week, dine out 5 and cook the other 3.

- Since dinner is typically more expensive than lunch, dine out for lunch and opt to cook dinner.

A financial strategy can help you save up to 40-50% of what you are spending dining out.

To understand the impact of your new strategy, reflect on the meals you had dining out:

- How did my body feel after eating those meals?

- How many times did I have leftovers for later?

- Could I have prepared similar meals at home?

By no means am I saying never dine out again! That would be preposterous. Dining out is an opportunity to try a variety of foods, connect with others, and practice self-care.

Think about the things you want to experience in life. Imagine saving an extra $5,000 a year for travel, investments, savings, education, or anything that you have been wanting to achieve. Small financial changes have a tremendous impact on your mind, body, and wallet.

▶ *The Takeaway:*

- Understanding eating habits helps you make sustainable decisions

- Cooking can create a space for bonding and relaxation

- Knowing spending habits helps you make more informed decisions about the future

Shall we talk about your "Why"?

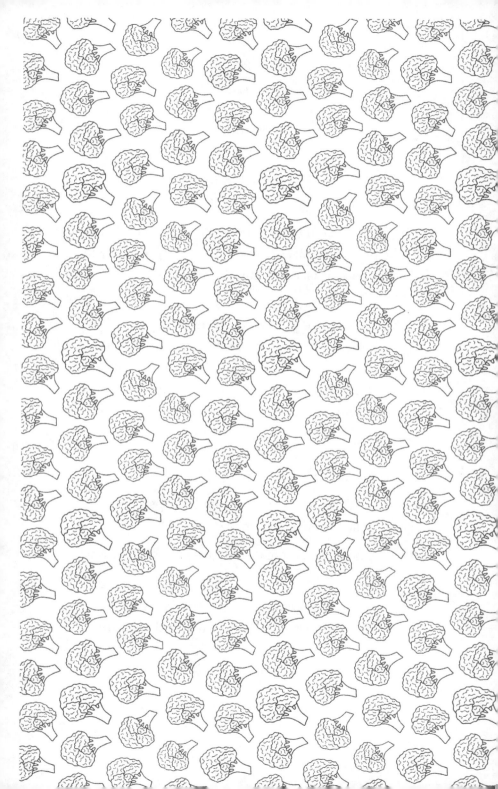

CHAPTER 3
You Are Why

I FOUND THE thought of a mustard green purely and utterly disgusting. It wasn't until adulthood that I found joy in the pungency. I experimented with various seasonings to bring out their flavor. I began to appreciate the benefits of their deep, green, rich color. This is an example of how digging deep helps you gain clarity on the foods you eat.

After the Nest, there is the opportunity to make your own food-related decisions. You hold the space to enjoy what you like, while learning to value foods you previously did not. Evaluate your "Whys" by asking:

Why do I stick with certain foods?

Why do I dislike particular foods?

Why does my body respond the way it does to some foods?

Ponder the foods you were fed as a baby bird. Determine why you loved them or even despised them. As a kid, my **Whys** were:

- **Taste**
- **Satisfaction**

As I used my Food Journal (you'll see this tool in the next chapter), I noticed my **Whys** began to shift. I identified foods that made me feel heavy and sleepy. I discovered the ones that kept me clear-headed, energized, and light. I felt stronger than ever. The more I journaled, the more intrigued I became.

The more I obeyed my body, the fewer sicknesses I experienced, like cold and flu. At this point, I finally understood what I live by to this day: **food is the best medicine ever.**

Today, my **Whys** are:

- **Taste**
- **Immunity**
- **Body feel**

▶ Intuition

Your body knows what's best for you. You'd be surprised how intuition guides your internal compass. The more in tune you are, the clearer your body can communicate its needs. As you get into alignment, allow intuition to be your guide.

Let's perform a meditation exercise. I bet you didn't anticipate meditation in a self-help cookbook, but here we go.

Take a moment to get relaxed. Close your eyes. Breathe slowly and deeply five times. Then ask your body:

- What do you desire of me?

- How may I serve you?

As you continue to breathe, make a mental note of the things revealed so you can incorporate them into your grocery list. Don't forget to thank your body for guidance.

▶ Simplicity

When starting out *After the Nest*, keep your first few dishes easy and relaxed. Choose a simple menu consisting of 1-2 dishes. I learned that throwing some of your favorite ingredients into one pot is a great way to gain cooking momentum.

Simplicity gives you the courage and confidence to advance to more challenging dishes. Need help coming up with recipes? I've loaned you some of my favorites (see the *After the Nest* Recipes in the appendix).

▶ *The Takeaway:*

- Eat what you enjoy
- Listen to your body
- When starting out, keep it simple

Now let's discuss that infamous word.

CHAPTER 4
The Infamous Word...

DIET (**NOUN**) – *the kind of food a person, animal, or community habitually eats.*

Every living thing has one. If you eat ice cream on a regular basis, you have an ice cream diet. If you eat whole-foods the majority of the time, then you have a whole-food diet.

Now you're probably thinking, "This is the part of the book where she tells me not to eat this or that". Nope.

After the Nest, you choose a diet that works for you. You decide which foods get access to your bloodstream. Knowledge of self is the beginning of your cooking path - and ultimately the root of all your food decisions. Start by asking the following:

Which foods do I eat often?

What foods are missing?

How do I feel after eating certain foods?

▶ Food Journal

Similar to a regular journal, a food journal can help you answer these questions. Journaling was truly the beginning of my food journey. For two months, I journaled what I ate. I was able to see the good (and not so good) of what I was and wasn't eating. This practice gave me a clear, honest picture of my eating habits.

Did I eat more or less on the weekends?

Was I overeating? Undereating?

Obtain the Food Journal from the appendix of this book.

▶ *How to Use a Food Journal*

Start by writing the day and date of your entry. Each day, log what you ate for breakfast, lunch, and dinner. Be sure to include any snacks and beverages. If you ate doughnuts for breakfast, write that. If you skipped a meal, write that too.

When documenting each day, note the following in your journal:

- Body feel (energized, light, heavy, groggy, etc.)

- Foods you enjoyed

- Cravings

- Whether the food was fast food or home-cooked

Here's an excerpt from my own Food Journal:

Day/Date	Wed, Nov 4
Breakfast	Fast food: Smoked sausage, egg, and cheese biscuit; hash browns, OJ
Lunch	Baked chicken sandwich; baked potato, sour cream, cheese
Dinner	Cereal, almond milk
Snack	Potato chips
Beverage	1 c water
Feeling	Sleepy, hungry
Notes	I cooked lunch. Had little water, no vegetables. Try again tomorrow.

Continue journaling for 1-2 months. Make observations as if conducting a lab experiment. Collect data without judgement. Remember, this is for your viewing only.

▶ *The Takeaway:*

- Gauge where you are in order to establish a starting point in your cooking path.

Let's gather an arsenal - without it, you'd probably go hungry.

CHAPTER 5
The Arsenal

I USED TO believe you had to buy a bunch of cookware just to start cooking. Not true. You can gradually add to your arsenal as you increase your culinary comfort zone. For now, you only need a few things. You can use this opportunity to align your cookware with your personality and taste.

Having an arsenal unique to you increases the likelihood of cooking *After the Nest*. I won't bore you with the details of purchasing a set of plates, bowls, spoons, forks, cups, etc., but I do want to encourage you to invest in these to prevent the overuse of paper products.

To help you figure out what you need for your arsenal, take a glance at your Food Journal. For example, if you see a theme of Chinese takeout, then your arsenal should reflect elements that allow you to cook Asian-inspired foods. Or if you're like me and breakfast is your absolute favorite meal, look into purchasing a griddle and spatula. These are a few examples to get the ball rolling in deciding your cookware.

Let's get to chopping.

▶ Cutting Board

There's something appealing about the rhythm of the chop-chop-chop sound on a cutting board. It has real chef appeal. Slicing and dicing can be quite addictive: a board allows you to practice and develop your knife skills.

With regard to safety, a cutting board reduces the possibility of injury. Cutting on a slick-surfaced plate can be a dangerous feat because the knife may slide towards your body. The bottom of the board provides the necessary traction to keep the board in place while cutting. The cutting surface also holds food in place. This allows for more control over the movement and direction of your knife.

You can opt for either a plastic cutting board or a wooden one. Plastic boards come in a variety of colors that can add flair to your kitchen decor. Wooden cutting boards add a natural aesthetic to your space. A decorative wooden board can double as a charcuterie board. Imagine the faces of your guests when you serve cheese, fruit, and crackers on your beautiful wooden board.

Now let's take a stab at knives
(oh, these knife puns are killing me).

▶ Knives

Keep in mind you don't have to break the bank by obtaining every type of knife ever created in the history of knives.

But first, let's revisit safety.

There are 3 factors that increase the risk of knife injury in the kitchen:

1. **Using a knife when distracted or when your senses are heightened (excited, angry):** Maintain a calm mind. Cut with focus and intention.

2. **Using an inappropriate knife:** Never use small knives to cut into large, hard, dense foods like a whole pineapple or raw potato, for example. Excessive force exerted onto a small knife is a setup for serious injury. When in doubt, use a Chef's Knife.

3. **Using a dull knife:** Dull knives also require excessive force to cut. Include a **Knife Sharpener** in your arsenal to ensure knives are sharp enough for the job at hand.

Remember, you only need a few essential knives to give you an edge (pun again) in the kitchen. Here are the most utilized:

▶ *Chef's Knife*

The perfect name for one of the most popular knives in the kitchen. Its long, curved blade makes it ideal for chopping, dicing, slicing, and mincing when used in conjunction with a cutting board. It's a star for meal prep. Find a blade length that works for you.

▶ *Paring Knife*

This knife's small size is beneficial for smaller fruits and vegetables. It is useful for precise cutting or peeling. Consider it the scalpel of your kitchen.

▶ *Kitchen Shears*

As a baby bird, I thought kitchen shears (aka food scissors) belonged in the junk drawer. Kitchen shears are one of the most under-utilized, but helpful tools in the kitchen. They can be used to cut meats into smaller portions or to cut into hard crustacean shells like the top portion of a lobster. Shears can also be used to quickly cut fresh herbs such as basil, chives, or parsley.

▶ Peeler

Another tool that makes kitchen life more appealing is a peeler. In contrast to using a paring knife, a peeler provides a more efficient means of removing more of the skin and less of the flesh (the tissue directly under the skin of a fruit or vegetable). As a result, more food ends up on your plate instead of the compost or garbage.

A peeler can also be used to create a Julienne cut. This involves cutting vegetables or fruit into ribbon-like strips. Since these cuts make the food smaller and less dense, less cooking time is required.

▶ Spatula

The spatula is a kitchen icon. If you're planning on cooking anything of a flat, round nature (pancakes, omelets, burgers, etc.), a Spatula is essential. Its flat, wide base slides under food so it can be flipped without breaking the food's intended form.

▶ *Tongs*

Now that we've flipped, let's grab! Tongs make it easy for grabbing and gently rotating girthy foods like steak or large, rounded vegetables (like an ear of corn). They allow you to pick up and put food down without dropping. They're also great for mixing and plating salads.

▶ *Bottle Opener*

Remember, not all bottles have twist-off caps. Enclosed corked bottles require a bottle opener. There's nothing like a dinner guest blessing you with a nice bottle of wine and you having nothing to open it - what a bummer.

▶ *Cooking Thermometer*

When it comes to ensuring food is cooked thoroughly, a cooking thermometer is necessary. Yes, you could cut into the thickest part of a chicken breast or steak to visually determine if it's cooked. However, having a thermometer ensures the required internal temperature has been reached to kill any present microbes. Check the packaging label for the appropriate cooking temperature. We'll discuss microbes later in more detail.

▶ *Measuring Devices*

Devices such as measuring cups, teaspoons, and tablespoons ensure the desired amount of a particular ingredient is in your recipe. They come in a variety of colors. You can also opt for wooden, plastic, glass, or metal measuring devices.

▶ Cookware

The same financial concept that applies to knives also applies to cookware. You don't need to make a huge investment to embark on your cooking journey - make selections based on your preference and taste buds. If you enjoy a certain style of cooking, purchase pieces that allow you to achieve that style.

Now before we dish (pun fun) on cookware, let's visit safety once more.

▶ *Fire Extinguisher*

Always have an accessible <u>chemical</u> Fire Extinguisher in the kitchen. These extinguishers are specifically designed to put out grease fires. Now that I look back, an extinguisher would have been a good idea for that deep fried liver scenario.

Moving right along. I introduce to you, the sauté pan.

▶ *Sauté Pan*

This type of pan has straight, low, flat sides and typically comes with a lid. The flat sides allow liquid to be maintained within the pan, minimizing evaporation during cooking. This creates a slow simmer which, in turn, invites a tenderness to the food. Foods cooked in sauté pans require moderate to much stirring.

These pans are great for marrying (marry = a process by which various flavor components within a container come together to create an improved flavor). Due to their high-sided design, these pans can also be used for deep frying - but let's keep the frying to a minimum. I'm sure you already know why, but we'll discuss in greater detail later.

If you're looking to keep your fat intake low, use water or broth as alternatives to oil. Using a non-stick sauté pan instead of oil is another option.

The next piece of cookware is often confused with the sauté pan. It is a wonderful piece to acquire and my personal favorite.

▶ *Skillet*

Skillets have wide, sloped sides. Based on how your skillet is used, a lid is optional. Its handle and sloped sides allow you to easily toss food around the pan. You can show off your flick of the wrist skills seen on the cooking channels. Skillets are great for cooking vegetables and small to medium cuts of meat.

The characteristics of the skillet are similar to another exciting piece of cookware invented in China over 2,000 years ago: the wok.

▶ *Wok*

A traditional wok has a wide, rounded bottom and requires a ring to sit in while cooking on the stove. Fortunately, woks have evolved to a flat bottom design, allowing it to sit directly on a stove top without a ring. As a result of its construction, heat distributes evenly and quickly. The wok's extremely high, wide, curved sides allow food to be easily tossed and evenly cooked. Woks may be purchased with or without a lid. Its design allows a minimal amount of cooking oil, while still achieving great taste.

This budget-friendly cookware is a good starter piece for new cooks. An entire meal can be prepared using only a wok; for example, they are great for quick, delicious, stir-fried meals (try the *Stir-Fry* recipe in the appendix). These meals can include almost any chopped vegetable, grain, protein (seafood, tofu, chicken, steak), and your favorite seasoning, sauce, or oil. Here's a bit of advice: *be sure to have your ingredients ready when you heat the wok.* Since it heats fast and cooks quick, your undivided attention is imperative.

▶ *Saucepan*

The saucepan is small in circumference and has straight, high sides with a long handle. It comes with a lid for maintaining or adjusting the temperature during the cooking process. As indicated by the name, saucepans are optimal for boiling small volumes and simmering sauces, pastas, and soups.

▶ *Stockpot*

For recipes that require large volumes of liquid, a stockpot is a necessity. It is a large, deep pot with tall sides, two handles, and a lid. It is used for boiling and stewing in large batches. A stockpot is awesome for preparing stews, sauces, and shellfish.

▶ *Crockpot*

Would you like the luxury of setting your food to cook and then going about your day? If so, the crockpot is just for you. Also known as a slow cooker, it is a countertop electrical appliance. It requires little attention, allowing food to simmer and cook at a low temperature over an extended period of time. The pot comes with a lid and consists of an inner container that sits inside a heating element. The crockpot contains feet to protect the supporting surface from its heat. Some are equipped with automatic shutoff timers.

The benefits of using a crockpot include the low cost of the appliance, simple meal preparation, minimal supervision, and large volume batch cooking. Slow cookers come in a variety of sizes and colors.

▶ Colander

A colander is a fancy name for a strainer. It is a two-handled, perforated bowl used to drain excessive liquids from solid foods after they cook. It's good for straining rice and pasta, as well as for rinsing fruit and vegetables. Colanders come in an array of colors and can be plastic or metal. A metal colander can also act as a food steamer over a boiling pot.

▶ Baking pans

Baking pans are popular for their pastry making qualities, but they can also double as a roasting or broiling pan to create savory vegetables or meats. Baking pans can be purchased in various materials including glass, metal, and stone, to name a few.

▶ *Air Fryer*

Air fryers have become another time-saving staple in the kitchen. Even though it's called a fryer, it requires little to no oil. A constant circulation of hot air gives the food a crusted coating, while maintaining the food's internal moisture appeal. It is not only beneficial for easy meal preparation and cleanup, but it requires little attention once it starts cooking. Air fryers come in a variety of sizes - see air fryer recipes in the appendix.

▶ *Griddle*

This is another one of my favorites. This electrical device has a broad, flat, metal plate cooking surface. Some can sit directly on the countertop while being used. They contain a trap that collects excessive grease or liquid that generates while cooking. A griddle can quickly adjust to temperature changes, which makes it great for cooking breakfasts foods like bacon, eggs, pancakes, or hash browns that may require various cooking temperatures. Their cooking surface makes for easy cleanup.

▶ *The Takeaway:*

- Having basic tools can set you in the right direction

- Cookware does not have to be expensive to bring success

Now let's discuss a topic I hope you never,
ever have to encounter.

CHAPTER 6
Mike Robes

I USED TO think the wonderful women who cooked for me were crazy clean freaks.

Don't get me wrong, I was by no means a slob. But it took a microbiology class to get my full attention. I finally understood that a few acts of carelessness here and there could mean a long visit to the bathroom… or, even worse, the Emergency Room. Their quest to keep a spotless kitchen finally made sense to me. I know I've harped on the concept that there are no right or wrongs when it comes to cooking, but in the case of safety, there are definitely rights and wrongs when it comes to food, microbes, and your health.

▶ Microbes

Microbes, or microorganisms, can thrive on unclean kitchen surfaces and utensils, in undercooked meat, and in food that is not stored at the recommended temperature. When ingested, some microbes can make you ill.

▶ *Tips/Takeaway:*

- I know this may be common sense, but I'll say it anyway. Wash your hands before cooking.

- Wash fruits and vegetables prior to consumption.

- Cook meat to the recommended internal temperature.

- Store foods in the recommended storage conditions.

- Sanitize hands, sinks, countertops, utensils, and any surfaces that come into contact with raw meat or raw eggs.

- To prevent cross-contamination to other utensils, use a dedicated container and utensils for raw meat and raw eggs.

- Refrigerate or freeze leftovers only after they cool (usually 2 hours after cooking).

Safety. Check! Now let's talk cheddar, cheese, dinero.

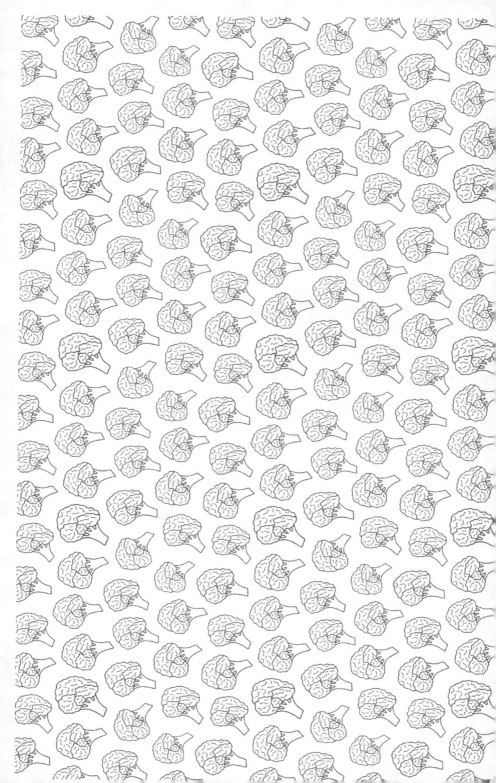

CHAPTER 7
Feast on a Budget

I USED TO think you had to spend a ton on groceries in order to eat well. Not true. Five-star restaurants don't pay outrageous amounts for the majority of their basic staples. What makes their food expensive is the experience, presentation, and, most importantly, the flavor. You can recreate all of these with your own foods.

In order to stay on track financially, it's important to know the following:

- How to make food delicious
- Which foods to buy and why
- Money saving tools

I'm going to go ahead and give you a takeaway for this chapter:

- **Smile at your bank account while eating deliciously and mindfully.**

▶ Seasonings, Oils, Sauces

This trio takes your cooking power from blah to BAM! Imagine turning simple, budget-friendly food into amazing food that happens to taste good <u>AND</u> be good for you.

▶ *Seasonings*

Basic seasonings like salt and pepper can bring food to life. Ponder the seasoning in your favorite foods or style of cooking, then collect them for your arsenal. Here are some examples:

- Mexican food: Cayenne, cumin, chili powder
- Italian foodies: Garlic, oregano, basil, bay leaves
- Indian cuisine: Curry, cumin, ginger, turmeric
- Grilling fans: Peppercorn, rosemary, thyme
- Seafood: Cajun spice, dill, smoked paprika

Seasonings such as herbs are not only cost and taste effective, but they can also be a boost to your health. Most contain zero to low calories. Seasonings like cumin, garlic, and ginger contain natural, healing components. The benefits are endless!

▶ *Sauces*

Sauces give food a rich, savory flavor while keeping you on track with your budget. Having condiments like mustard, ketchup, mayonnaise, and a variety of salad dressings on hand is a plus.

The principle of seasonings can also be applied to sauces. Again, ponder your favorite meals and curate the sauces used to create them.

- Mexican food: Salsa, siracha, chili-lime

- Italian: Marinara, alfredo sauce, pesto

- Grilling: Barbecue sauce, steak sauce, marinades

- Seafood: Cocktail sauce, dill sauce, tartar sauce, fresh lemon juice

- Asian meals: Teriyaki sauce, soy sauce, peanut sauce, wasabi

Get creative. Mix things up. Combining seasons with sauces is phenomenal. As you advance in your cooking, your palate may evolve to new flavors. Even the most seasoned (another pun) chefs get excited about flavors they experience for the first time.

▶ *Oils*

Oils give a richness and texture to food. Quality oils can be on the pricey side, but a small amount can go a long way. Plant oils such as avocado, sesame, coconut, and grapeseed oils are great for cooking. Extra virgin olive oil (or EVOO) is great for salad dressings. When oils are consumed in small amounts, they contribute to the absorption of vitamins D, A, K, and E in the body.

Keep low quality, animal fat oils at a minimum. An excessive intake of these oils tends to clog the arteries, which can lead to heart disease or stroke.

▶ Whole or Processed Food?

▶ *Proce$$ed Food*

Disclaimer: This is by no means a bashing session on processed foods. When eaten in moderation, they can be enjoyable. But in excess, they can wreak havoc on your mind and body.

What does the term "processed" mean?

- Food chemically altered from its natural state

- Food not found in nature

Many processed foods contain refined sugars and preservatives to extend freshness. Artificial colors and flavors are added to enhance food appearance and taste. Its outer packaging, such as plastic, foil, or cardboard, is a major contributor to its hefty price tag, not to mention the impact the packaging waste has on the ecosystem.

▶ *Whole Food*

The more whole foods you consume, the cheaper your grocery bill will be. Don't believe me?

Next time you grocery shop, take a glance at your receipt. Notice your whole foods (fruits, vegetables, bulk grains) are far cheaper than your pre-packaged foods (frozen meals, boxed food, etc.). Whole foods are cheaper because they require less packaging, handling, and are free of expensive additives.

When you make whole foods the majority of your food, you do a great service to your body, mind, budget, and environment. When it comes to purchasing whole foods, there are options: fresh, frozen, or canned.

▶ Fresh, Frozen, or Canned

▶ *Fresh Food*

Fresh whole foods come directly from the plant or farm. They are the cheapest and healthiest form of eating. Because they're in their natural state, you maximize the benefits you get from them.

Even though the grocery store offers whole foods, try shopping at a local farm when possible. This is an environmentally sound option based on the following:

- There is minimal food transport from the local farm to you. A reduction in transport fuel usage decreases its harmful effects on the environment.

- Whole foods require little to zero outer packaging, which equates to less waste in the environment.

▶ *Frozen Food*

Frozen foods are a great option for keeping your whole foods a little longer than their fresh counterparts. This, in turn, reduces spoilage and waste. Most frozen foods are cooked, then frozen. This processing can cause the food to lose a few vitamins and minerals.

However, frozen foods are still a good option to give your body what it needs while maintaining a budget.

▶ *Canned Food*

Canned foods can also be stored longer than fresh foods. However, keep in mind that canned foods may contain preservatives, additives, and a high level of salt or added sugar. Be aware of canned food ingredients by reading their label. We'll get more into reading labels later, but first, let's discuss another aspect of the budget: **organics and non-organics**.

▶ To Organic or Not Organic?

You've probably heard over and over again that purchasing organic foods is the best route for your health. Yes, organic foods have their advantages, but it can be challenging for your budget *After the Nest*. Here's why.

Foods labeled organic cannot contain chemical agents such as pesticides and growth hormones. These agents can be harmful to the body if consumed often. Organic cropping without using these agents requires more work for the farmer to grow food to the optimal size, while also keeping pests away. As a result, you pay more for the farmer's additional labor to yield an organic product.

▶ *Non-Organic*

All hope is not lost. There are some foods that do not hold an organic status, but can still be consumed safely. Allow me to explain.

My local farmer uses an anti-pest agent on his crops. This agent dissipates before the food makes it to me. There are even some plants that naturally produce their own anti-pest material.

There is information available that can help you decide whether to purchase organic or non-organic. Check out the guidance lists published by the FDA and USDA regulated **Environmental Working Group** (ewg.org). This non-profit organization was created to protect the consumer and the environment. Their lists are updated annually, so be sure to obtain a current list of the following:

- **The Clean 15**: A list of 15 fruits and vegetables that contain low amounts of pesticides. These foods can be purchased non-organic.

- **The Dirty Dozen**: A list of 12 fruits and vegetables that contain high levels of pesticides. It is my recommendation to buy these foods organic when possible.

▶ Money Saving Tools

After the Nest, I started couponing here and there. I noticed how the savings began to add up. Traditional paper coupons can still be used, but grocers have made it convenient by offering digital coupons. There are also grocery stores that give automatic discounts for being a loyal customer! Download your favorite grocer's app to save money, time, and paper.

▶ *The Takeaway:*

- For taste and flavor, experiment with seasonings, sauces, and oils.

- Do a little research.

- Get acquainted with local farmers to find out about their pest management and grow practices.

- Adopt a financial shopping strategy that works for you.

Now that you have the tools to create your grocery list, let's get the goods.

Then God said,

"I've given you every sort of seed-bearing plant on Earth, and every kind of fruit-bearing tree, given them to you for food. To all animals and all birds, everything that moves and breathes, I give whatever grows out of the ground for food."

— **Genesis 1:29-30**

CHAPTER 8
How to Shop It

▶ Step 1: Avoid shopping on an empty stomach

hunger + a store full of food = desperate impromptu purchases

This can quickly and easily happen when you're unprepared. Try eating a meal or snack prior to going into the grocery store. This principle can apply to online shopping as well! Yes, a few indulgences may wind up in your cart, but it's okay. You still have a plan in hand. And that plan is your grocery list.

▶ Step 2: Have a grocery list

Have you ever wandered into the grocery store, struggled to remember what you came for, grabbed things you already have, forgotten the things you needed, and then wound up having to turn around and go back to the same store?

A grocery list not only helps you remember what to buy, but it also helps save time and money. But, most importantly, it keeps indulgences in check while helping you stay on course with your **Whys**.

▶ Step 3: Map it out

▶ *First Stop: The Produce Section*

By starting in this area, you set the tone for the rest of your shopping. Placing fruits and vegetables in your cart first can influence mindful decisions for the rest of your selections, even if you plan on indulging a little.

The produce section is typically located at the front of most stores. Why? The grocer wants you to buy these perishables so they don't sit and rot on their shelves.

Try to select a range of colors in your fruits and vegetables. Color indicates the presence of nutrients. The more colors you consume, the better the chance of your body getting what it needs without you having to put much thought into it.

Imagine a salad bowl with red tomatoes, vibrant orange carrots, yellow bell peppers, lush green spinach, blueberries, and beets. Remember, **Roy G Biv**.

Red **o**range **y**ellow **G**reen **B**lue **i**ndigo **v**iolet

▶ *Second Stop: The Center Aisles*

Center aisles contain the most expensive, processed, packaged, salty, sugary, fat-ladened stuff out of all the sections in the store. Navigate this area mindfully.

It's important to read labels on the products in this section of the store. Get familiar with their contents and their potential impact on your body. Reading labels is explained in further detail in the next chapter.

These aisles have good stuff in them too. They contain staples such as grains, sauces, seasonings, and dressings that add a flavorful touch to your meals.

▶ *Last Stop: Temperature-Controlled Foods*

If your grocery list involves meat, dairy, frozen, or in-store cooked items, make these selections last. This is to ensure they are at their coldest (or warmest) when you leave the store. *Food safety and quality are key.*

▶ *The Takeaway:*

- Have a plan
- Have a list
- Shop in color

CHAPTER 9
Labels 101

"I'm only gonna eat a handful and that's it".

— Me, The lies I tell myself about potato chips

I literally fall short every time.

Did you know that many of your favorite food manufacturers invest millions in researching your eating habits? Countless hours and studies are used to perfect how your food looks and tastes. Some manufacturers use control groups to ascertain a way to create an addiction. This is why it is important to know what's in your food.

After the Nest, I paid no attention to food labels. I would nonchalantly pick up food containers and toss them in my cart. Becoming a Health Coach brought awareness to the importance of reading and understanding food labels.

▶ Nutrition Fact Label

It's crucial to know exactly what and how much of a thing goes into your food – and, ultimately, your body. The Nutrition Fact Label communicates this information. It brings awareness to what a food is comprised of in order for the consumer to make an informed decision about that product.

▶ Sugars & Their Aliases

Sugar can have a great impact on your health. It is added to many packaged foods and goes by many names. Overconsumption of these sugars can increase the risk of obesity, diabetes, some cancers, heart disease, dental cavities, and inflammation. This makes it even more critical for you to be aware of their aliases and disguises.

Just to be clear, added sugars and natural sugars are not the same. Natural sugars are present in fruits, some vegetables, and some dairy products. Added sugars are exactly what their name implies. They are added to sweeten and/or preserve food.

Tip: All sugars, whether natural or added, should be consumed in moderation.

Now let's do a little experiment. Go to your refrigerator or pantry. Glance at a few of your food labels. Look for ingredients that say:

- High fructose corn syrup
- Fruit juice concentrate
- Honey
- Syrup
- Molasses
- Words ending in "ose"

These are all added sugars.

▶ Added Sugar Amount

The current Nutrition Facts Label specifies the **Total Amount** of sugar (natural + added). In this total, the label further clarifies the amount of added sugar in a serving. When it comes to servings, sometimes you get more than you think. More is not always good. Take soda, for example.

▶ Serving Size

Many sodas contain more than one serving per bottle. Let's say there are 23 grams of sugar in one serving. If you drink an entire bottle that contains two servings, you would have consumed 46 grams (or 11 teaspoons) of sugar. That far exceeds the daily limit of sugar, which is typically 20-22 grams depending on your body. From our previous discussion, we already know the ramifications of a high sugar intake.

If you must have soda:

- Drink a glass of water between each serving
- Share your beverage
- Opt for a single serving bottle

▶ Artificial Preservatives

Preservatives are added to processed foods to prolong their freshness. Without preserving agents, most foods would quickly spoil while sitting on grocery store shelves. This loss would be costly to the grocer and the manufacturer – and, ultimately, costly to you.

A high intake of synthetic preservatives such as sodium benzoate, sulfites, and nitrates may contribute to health issues such as asthma, Alzheimer's, and even cancer.

Preservatives such as salt, some sugars, vinegar, and citric acid derive from a natural state. It is recommended to make these preservatives the preferred option.

▶ Artificial Colors

Artificial colors add color or help maintain a food's natural color. Have you ever heard the phrase "Eat with your eyes"? There is a certain enticement color brings to the taste buds.

For example, farm-raised salmon is not naturally pink, but more of a grayish color. But who really wants to eat "Gray Salmon"? An artificial colorant is added to make farm-raised salmon appear like its wild, naturally pink counterpart.

When consumed frequently and in high amounts, artificial colors can lead to ADHD or allergic reactions.

When reading food labels, be aware of ingredients whose name starts with a color and ends with a number. For example, Yellow No. 5 is used to color some sodas, chips, cereals, and candy. Red No. 40 is used in some sports drinks and condiments.

On the label, go for natural colors like beta carotene (think sweet potatoes, carrots, or pumpkins), anthocyanin (think reds and blues from berries), beet extract (for a deep purple color), and turmeric (for yellow coloring).

▶ Artificial Flavors

We'll end the artificial section tastefully (the puns continue) with flavors. Flavors intensify the taste and smell of what some may consider drab foods. Artificial flavors carry similar health risks to those of artificial preservatives and colors. Natural flavors such as vanilla bean, mustard seed, or dill seed derive from natural sources. Go for the natural stuff.

▶ Ingredients List

As you grocery shop, take a moment to read the ingredients section of the Nutrition Fact Labels. The first 2-3 ingredients listed make up the majority of that food.

Stick with simple ingredients you can pronounce. Gravitate to the ones you're familiar with. If you're unsure of a particular ingredient, use your device to research it.

▶ *The Takeaway:*

- Gravitate toward familiar ingredients
- Choose more foods that do not require a Nutrition Fact Label
- Be aware of the artificial stuff
- Know the number of servings in your packaged foods

Who's ready to cook?

CHAPTER 10
How to Cook It

YOU KNOW YOU like certain foods, but with so many cooking methods out there, where does one start? To help you decide, ponder the following:

- What food did I enjoy eating in the nest?
- What have I always wanted to try cooking?
- Which cooking method am I comfortable experimenting with?

Sidenote: Remember to also get into a habit of throwing raw vegetables and fruits on your plate. This is great for digestion.

And always remember: keep it simple and have fun.

▶ Sautéing

Sautéing is my favorite cooking method. It's safe, quick, and easy qualities make it one of the best options for new chefs. Sautéing is different from frying because it involves a smaller, shallower amount of oil. This means less hot grease popping and a less lingering fried food scent.

This method is preferable for cooking small pieces of food. Sautéing at a medium-high temperature can create a brown, but not burnt, crust on food. This crusting is called caramelization. The use of sauces and seasonings intensifies caramelization, creating a rich, flavorful food.

Reminder: Water, broth, or non-stick sautéing pans can be used in place of oil to sauté.

See my **Sautéed Shrooms N' Spinach** recipe in the appendix.

▶ Roasting

This method is a great starting point for new cooks. It involves simple preparation and moderate monitoring. This style of cooking is great for those who like to eat multiple times from one large meal. Ingredients can be prepped whole or cut into smaller pieces. To enhance flavor, use herbs, oil, seasoning, or sauce.

Roasting is ideal for cooking whole, dense vegetables like carrots, potatoes, eggplants, or thick meats like a roast or whole chicken.

This slow cooking method circulates dry heat from the bottom of the oven and cooks upward. Cooking time depends on the type and size of your food. The use of oil helps prevent sticking to the roasting pan. Sticking can also be prevented by using non-stick foil or a non-stick pan. Roasting is a healthy form of cooking because it maintains nutrients in food. Check out the **Roasted Buffalo Wings** recipe in the appendix.

▶ Broiling

Broiling uses high temperature dry heat. In contrast to roasting, broil heat originates from the top of the oven and cooks downward. This causes food to cook extremely fast. Close attention is imperative. Ensure the roasting pan surface is non-stick or the food is moderately coated with oil.

Broiling is great for small or cut vegetables and small portions of meat. Seasonings and sauces help create a flavorful crust or sear on broiled foods. Try the **Spicy Broiled Salmon** recipe in the appendix.

▶ Slow Cooking (Crockpot)

As society becomes more and more fast-paced, a time-saving method like slow cooking is essential. A crockpot provides the flexibility of creating delicious, healthy meals while you sleep or work. This cooking process gives food a tender, flavorful composition, making it optimal for stews and soups. I just happen to have a recipe for **Crockpot Chili** in the appendix.

▶ Frying

This method of cooking involves using hot oil. Frying gives food a crispy, seared, or caramelized outer layer. There are several frying methods.

Stir-frying involves using a skillet or wok and requires a small amount of oil (think tablespoons) to coat the pan's surface.

Pan frying involves immersing about two-thirds of the foods surface area into a shallow amount of oil (think cups of oil) in a sauté pan. Remember the aforementioned deep-fried liver? Pan frying would have been the optimal cooking method in that scenario.

Deep frying involves completely submerging food into a large amount of oil (think liters of oil).

Eating deep fried foods on a frequent basis can contribute to high blood pressure, clogged arteries, and high cholesterol. **Use frying methods in moderation.**

Prior to preparing your first meal, you may experience some hesitation, nervousness, or excitement. All of these feelings are perfectly okay. They are indicators that you're ready to embark on a habit that will sustain you for the rest of your life. And I hope your first meal is a wreck!

You're probably thinking, "Did I read that correctly? She hopes my first meal is a wreck? What kind of crap is that to say?" No, that was not a typo.

Just get it out of the way already! That moment will always be memorable to you (i.e. bloody liver). It'll give you opportunity to laugh with yourself, to grow, and to try again. Take the pressure off. Don't take this moment too serious. Know that whatever you create is perfect because it came from you, Baby Bird.

▶ *The Takeaway:*

- Tweak recipes to your liking.
- Have fun with whatever cooking method you try.

With that being said, let's showoff a masterpiece.

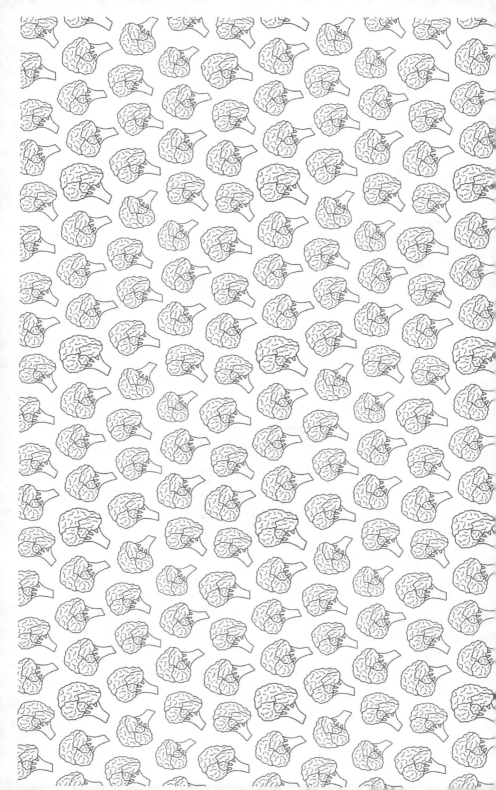

CHAPTER II
A Whiff of a Masterpiece

MY GRANDMOTHER USED to say, "It's all going to the same place". No doubt about that. If you're ready to feast, by all means toss that food on a plate and have at it! But if you really want to take your food game up a notch, throw in some aesthetics. It's quite impressive. Allow me to paint a picture.

Imagine being at a five-star restaurant. The dessert arrives to your neighboring table. You notice the red glaze drizzled over the sides of the cheesecake onto the plate. You swoon over the fresh strawberries and thickness of the graham cracker crust. Even the green mint leaf catches your eye. Just describing this scenario makes my mouth water.

This is the effect of food aesthetics, or food artistry. Imagine your plate a blank canvas, awaiting to be decorated with a medium of your own food. As you can see in my attempt at imagery above, food can be orchestrated to create a craving. The sight of appealing food can stimulate the salivary glands. The digestion process begins in your mind before putting a morsel of food into your mouth.

While there are many ways to make your plate beautiful, we'll focus on two simple techniques: plating and garnishing.

▶ Plating

Plating involves arranging your food in an organized, decorative manner. Think about it like this: when people are impressed by the appearance of their plated food, most times they'll take a few seconds to savor the moment before digging in. Many even take a picture of it.

Plating can involve:

- Drizzling sauce so it flows from one food to the other
- Stacking food
- Using special serving dishes and utensils
- Ensuring the exposed parts of your serving dish are clean and sparkly.

Plating shows care for your effort, gives appreciation to those you may be serving, and demonstrates gratitude for the food itself.

▶ Garnishing

Garnishing involves decorating food with smaller foods. Here are some examples:

- Parmesan shaved over spaghetti topped with a basil leaf

- Balsamic glaze drizzled over tomatoes and mozzarella

- Sprinkles of parsley over your food and plate

- Sliced peaches and honey atop oatmeal

- Toasted sesame seeds scattered over stir-fry

- Almond slivers and cinnamon on a hot sweet potato

- Pieces of candy bar and chunks of fresh strawberries over a scoop of vanilla ice cream

The combinations and possibilities are endless. Be bold. Create your masterpiece.

▶ Aromatics

This is the "whiff" part of the chapter. Aromas are also powerful in food appeal; they excite the tastebuds with a preview of what's to come. Olfactory organs play a major role in the beginning stages of digestion.

The smell of food can also evoke memories. The scent of vanilla and nutmeg remind me of my grandmother's baked sweet potato pies. I would quietly, but excitedly, wait to devour the remnants of her mixing bowl. Do you have any scent induced memories?

▶ *The Takeaway:*

- Allow your plate to be your work of art
- Bask in the beauty and aroma of your food

CHAPTER 12
New Traditions

WHILE IN THE nest, my mother would play music while she cooked. I hold to this tradition because it ushers in my cooking energies - not to mention the dancing that may occur.

Did you have any traditions as a Baby Bird?

Are there new traditions you can establish as a Fledgling?

Here are a few ideas:

- Take leftovers to (or cook for) someone in need

- Share your meal with a friend who has little time to cook due to extenuating circumstances

- Inspire someone to start their food journey by sharing recipes or cooking experiences.

- Take a pic and start a food gallery.

  o   If you're comfortable, share your photos with the world. Social media eats food pics up (there's a pun).

▶ *The Takeaway:*

- Pay homage to old traditions while creating new ones

- Inspire

- Pay it forward

CLOSING REMARKS

I'M VERY PROUD of you. I hope you're proud of yourself.

My prayer is that the knowledge you gain from this book inspires you and generations to come. I also hope that it guides you into a life-long path of memorable, adventurous, free-spirited cooking.

Remember, you got this!

Above all, remember **Option C.**

APPENDIX I
After the Nest Food Journal

Day/Date	
Breakfast	
Lunch	
Dinner	
Snack	
Beverages	
Body feel after eating	
Note	

Day/Date	
Breakfast	
Lunch	
Dinner	
Snack	
Beverages	
Body feel after eating	
Note	

Day/Date	
Breakfast	
Lunch	
Dinner	
Snack	
Beverages	
Body feel after eating	
Note	

APPENDIX II
After the Nest Recipes

Before we dive in…

Feel free to experiment with these recipes.

When you're ready, feel free to substitute ingredients to make these recipes your own.

You'll see the phrase *"to taste"* next to some of the ingredients. This means as you cook, taste the food and adjust that ingredient to your liking.

Bon Appetit!

OVERNIGHT POWER OATS

½ cup old-fashion oats

1 pinch raisins

1 tsp chia seeds

1 tsp protein powder

1 palmful nuts of your choice   (optional)

1 dash salt

1 dash cinnamon

1 dash ginger powder

1 c almond milk

Place ingredients in a mason jar, adding milk last. Add lid and shake jar vigorously to mix. Refrigerate 3-8 hours. Shake jar. Top with fresh fruit of your choice.

Tip: Option to use any other nut milk, water, or whole milk.

Tip: Banana, blueberries, strawberries, or apple make for great toppings.

SHRIMP STIR FRY

1 lb. shrimp (deveined, shell off)

½ onion (sliced)

2 c broccoli florets

1 carrot (julienned)

4 mushrooms (sliced)

3 bunches baby bok choy

2 cloves garlic (peeled, sliced)

½ c teriyaki sauce

¼ c sesame oil

¼ c toasted sesame seeds

½ red bell pepper (sliced)

1 zucchini (sliced)

In a wok, heat 2 tablespoons of oil over medium heat. Add mushrooms, onions, broccoli, carrots, bell pepper, zucchini, garlic, and teriyaki sauce, stirring often. Cook vegetables to desired consistency.

Remove content and place in a separate container.

Do not clean the wok, but add remaining oil and shrimp. Halfway cooking the shrimp (one side is opaque), add in the cooked vegetables and bok choy. Continue until shrimp is fully cooked (fully opaque).

To plate, place stir fry over rice of your choice and garnish with sesame seeds.

Tip: Substitute shrimp with protein of your choice.

And if you're feeling saucy

...A LITTLE SOY SAUCE NEVER HURT ANYBODY

SWEET POTATO FRIES WITH HONEY CITRUS DIP

1 large sweet potato (skinned, cut into strips)

1 tbs grapeseed oil

1 large pinch of sugar

Cooking spray

Spray air fryer tray with cooking spray. Toss potatoes in grapeseed oil and air fry on 390° F for 15 min (additional time may be needed for thicker cut potato strips). Remove and sprinkle with sugar.

HONEY CITRUS DIP:

1 oz honey

2 tbsp fresh lemon juice

Warm honey in microwave for 5-6 seconds. Place honey in ramakin and stir in the lemon juice.

GOURMET TURKEY BURGERS

1 lb. ground turkey

2 tbs onion (diced)

¼ cup bell pepper (diced)

2 mushrooms (diced)

1 large clove garlic (peeled, sliced)

1 pinch dried rosemary

1 tsp chili powder

½ tsp seasoned salt

Mix all ingredients in a bowl. Divide mixture into four parts. Form each part into a patty. Spray air fryer tray with cooking spray and air fry patties at 385°F for 13 – 15 min.

Tip: Prepare toasted wheat bread or multi-grain burger bun with sriracha mayo, fresh spinach, and tomato.

Tip: Pair burger with **Red Potato Fries with Dill Ketchup Dip** recipe.

RED POTATO FRIES WITH DILL KETCHUP DIP

4 red potatoes, cut into ½ inch thick wedges

1 tbsp avocado oil

1 dash sea salt

1 dash pepper

Cooking spray

Spray air fryer tray with cooking spray. Toss potatoes in oil and air fry at 385°F for 15 min. Shake wedges around air fryer container halfway into the cooking time. Remove and sprinkle with salt. Garnish with parsley.

Dill Ketchup Dip:

1 oz ketchup

1 tbsp dill pickles cubes (minced)

Mix ketchup and diced dill pickles.

SPICY BROILED SALMON

2 salmon (fillet)

1 tbsp whole grain mustard

1 tbsp dill pickle cubes (minced)

1 tbsp smoked paprika

1 tbsp siracha mayo

½ tsp salt

½ tsp pepper

Rinse and pat salmon dry. Season with salt and pepper. Line baking pan with foil and place salmon skin side down.

Mix mustard, paprika, pickles, and mayo in a bowl. Coat the top and sides of salmon with mixture.

Broil on low for 6-8 minutes, then broil on high for 2-3 minutes until the top of the salmon containing the mixture turns dark gold. Use a cooking thermometer to ensure salmon is thoroughly cooked. Additional cooking time may be needed for larger pieces of salmon.

ALL THINGS TURKEY CHILI

1 lb. ground turkey

1- 24 oz tomato sauce

1- 10 oz canned tomatoes

1 onion (quartered)

3 cloves garlic (peeled, chopped)

1 bell pepper (chunks)

2 zucchini (thick sliced)

3 bay leaves

Dried oregano (to taste)

Salt (to taste)

Pepper (to taste)

Sugar (to taste)

¼ c grapeseed oil

1 can black beans (rinsed, drained)

Heat two tablespoons of oil over medium heat in a skillet. Cook ground turkey and drain. In a crockpot, add turkey, onion, bell pepper, garlic, canned tomatoes, tomato sauce, oregano, salt, pepper, bay leaves, and sugar. Set crockpot on low and cook for 6-8 hours. Add beans at the last hour of cooking.

For faster cooking time, set crockpot on high and cook for 3-4 hours. Minimal stirring is necessary during the cooking process.

Tip: Chili can be enjoyed by itself or as a taco salad over mixed greens. Try serving it on top of your favorite pasta.

GARNISH WITH FRESH GRATED PARMESAN CHEESE.

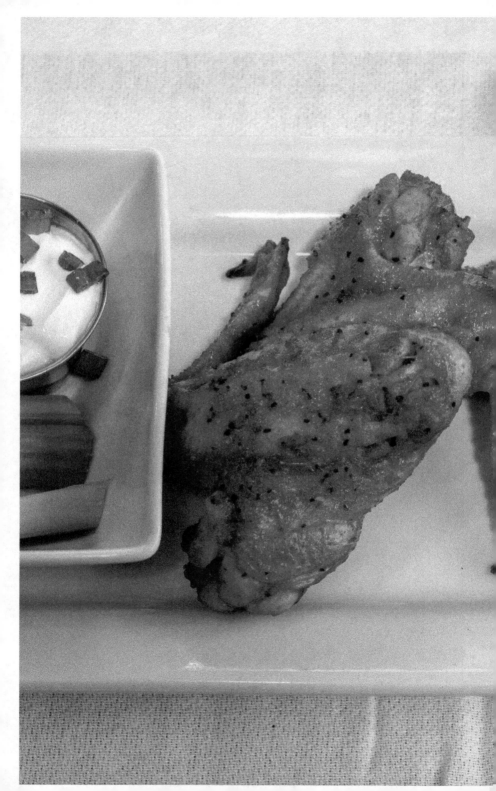

ROASTED BUFFALO WINGS

1 lb. chicken wings

1 tbs lemon pepper

½ tsp seasoned salt

1 c buffalo sauce

½ c butter (melted)

Toss wings in butter and buffalo sauce. Add lemon pepper and salt. Place wings in a foil pouch, enclose, and place on a baking sheet. Bake for 30-40 minutes, flipping them over halfway through the cooking time. Open the pouch and broil on high for 3 min.

Dip: Serve with ranch Greek yogurt or blue cheese dressing.

SAUTÉED SHROOMS N' SPINACH

1 c baby spinach

1 clove garlic (sliced)

2 portobello mushrooms

½ tsp liquid amino soy sauce

½ tsp turmeric powder

1 tbsp avocado oil

Heat oil on medium heat in a skillet. Add mushrooms to pan and cook for 30 seconds. Add spinach, garlic, soy sauce, and turmeric. Cook for 1-2 minutes.

Tip: Add in a chopped boiled egg for protein.

ABOUT THE AUTHOR

Coach Antoinette L. Beeks

Integrative Nutrition Wellness Coach Antoinette L. Beeks, author of After The Nest, is no stranger to great cooking. An avid foodie and aspiring culinary therapy chef, this Greenville South Carolina native and inhabitant of Charleston is no stranger to excellent food. As a child, she was always intrigued by the fundamentals of the human body. This led her to pursue an undergraduate degree in Biology from Charleston Southern University. Even though she hailed from a family of well-rounded cooks, she faced the real-world post grad challenge of not knowing how to cook. Using faith to help her breakthrough these obstacles, she unknowingly developed a blueprint for simple, healthy, feel-good cooking. The side effect of this blueprint was the loss of an excessive 50 pounds.

Over a decade later, she uses this same approach to maintain this improved state of health and vitality. Antoinette went on to earn her Integrative Nutrition Health Coaching certification from the Institute for Integrative Nutrition. She inspires others to mesh eating and being well with simple, yet delicious food. Volunteering with the senior resources division at Meals on Wheels gives her a deep gratitude for people and food. Working in the corporate arena, she had the opportunity to teach the employment sector ways to implement their own wellness strategies, while maintaining demanding careers. She enjoys spending time with her family, travel, drumming, indoor cycling, the calming nature of the ocean, and of course great cuisine.

CPSIA information can be obtained
at www.ICGtesting.com
Printed in the USA
JSHW070911191222
33901JS00006B/5

9 780578 333656